The 2024 Vision:
A Comprehensive Guide to Achieving Your Goals.

TABLES OF CONTENTS

Introduction:
- Explain why you decided to write the book.
- Discuss the importance of setting goals in various life domains.
- Provide an overview of what the book will cover.

Chapter 1: The Philosophy of Goal Setting
- Discuss the psychological basis of goal setting.
- Explain the SMART criteria (Specific, Measurable, Achievable, Relevant, Time-bound).
- Talk about the importance of motivation and vision.

Chapter 2: Health - The Foundation of Success
- Importance of health for overall well-being and productivity.
- Detailed plans for incorporating exercise, nutrition, sleep, and stress management into daily life.
- Personal anecdotes or success stories.

Chapter 3: Wealth - Securing Your Future
- The role of financial stability in personal development.
- Step-by-step guidance on budgeting, saving, investing, and debt management.
- Include worksheets or templates for financial planning.

Chapter 4: Relationships - The Bonds That Shape Us
- Discuss the impact of personal relationships on happiness and success.
- Provide strategies for improving communication, showing appreciation, and building connections.
- Share exercises for conflict resolution and deepening relationships.

Chapter 5: Career - Crafting Your Path
- Emphasize career planning and professional growth.
- Offer advice on education, skill development, networking, and work-life balance.
- Include interviews or case studies of successful career advancements.

Chapter 6: Spirituality - The Inner Journey
- Explore the importance of spiritual well-being and its influence on other life areas.
- Provide guidance for meditation, mindfulness, and community involvement.
- Share your own spiritual journey or others' experiences.

Chapter 7: Bringing It All Together
- Discuss how to integrate goals across different life domains.
- Stress the importance of balance and flexibility in goal pursuit.
- Provide a yearly or monthly plan to achieve goals, including regular reflection and adjustment.

Chapter 8: Overcoming Obstacles
- Address common challenges and setbacks in goal achievement.
- Share strategies for staying motivated and overcoming procrastination.
- Offer advice on dealing with failure and learning from experiences.

Chapter 9: Tools and Resources
- Provide a list of apps, books, websites, and other resources to assist in achieving goals.
- Discuss the role of technology in tracking and supporting goal progress.

Introduction:
Embracing the Journey of Personal Transformation

Welcome to "The 2024 Vision: A Comprehensive Guide to Achieving Your Goals," a holistic roadmap to not just dreaming about the life you want but actively crafting it with your own hands. This book is a testament to the belief that within each of us lies the potential for greatness, the resilience to overcome adversity, and the creativity to forge our path.

As we stand on the brink of 2024, you might feel a mix of excitement and uncertainty about the future. Whether you're looking to enhance your well-being, secure your financial future, deepen your relationships, advance your career, or nourish your spiritual life, the coming year is a canvas waiting for your brushstrokes.

<u>Why a book about goals?</u> Because goals are the waypoints on the journey to a fulfilled life. They give us direction, motivate us to push through challenges, and serve as benchmarks for our progress. But setting goals is just the beginning. The true magic lies in the pursuit – the daily decisions, habits, and attitudes that inch us closer to our aspirations.

In this book, we'll dive deep into five critical areas of life: Health, Wealth, Relationships, Career, and Spirituality. Each chapter will provide you not only with the rationale behind setting specific goals in these domains but also with a practical, step-by-step guide on how to achieve them. You'll find strategies tested by time, endorsed by experts, and, most importantly, designed for the real world.

Let's embark on this transformative journey together. By the end of this book, you will have a clear plan for 2024 and the tools to adapt and thrive in the years that follow. So, turn the page, and let's step into a year of growth, achievement, and self-discovery.

<u>Chapter 1:</u> The Philosophy of Goal Setting

Psychological Basis of Goal Setting

Goal setting is a powerful process for thinking about your ideal future and for motivating yourself to turn your vision of this future into reality. The psychological basis of goal setting lies in several theories and principles. One of the foundational theories is ***Edwin Locke's Goal-Setting Theory***, which suggests that goal setting is intrinsically linked to task performance.

Locke's theory postulates that specific and challenging goals, along with appropriate feedback, lead to higher performance. The act of setting goals is believed to influence our internal psychological state by:

1. Directing our attention to the relevant activities and away from irrelevant ones.
2. Mobilizing our energy and efforts, leading to heightened work intensity.
3. Increasing our persistence, so we are more likely to follow through.

4. Fostering the development of strategies and action plans that facilitate goal attainment.

Moreover, the process of setting and working towards goals can enhance our sense of self-efficacy and provide a source of internal satisfaction once goals are achieved.

SMART Criteria

The SMART criteria are a guide for setting clear and reachable goals. It stands for:

- **Specific:** Goals should be clear and specific, so you know exactly what you're working towards. This clarity reduces the ambiguity of what is to be achieved.
- **Measurable:** Goals should have criteria for measuring progress. If a goal is measurable, it's easier to track progress and know when it has been accomplished.
- **Achievable:** Goals should be realistic and attainable. While challenging goals can be motivating, they also need to be set within the bounds of possibility.
- **Relevant:** Goals should be relevant to the direction you want your life or work to take. A relevant goal will align with other goals and fit within your immediate and long-term plans.
- **Time-bound:** Goals need a target date so that there's a deadline to focus on and something to work toward. This part of the SMART criteria helps to prevent everyday tasks from taking priority over your longer-term goals.

Importance of Motivation and Vision:

Motivation and vision are critical components of successful goal setting and achievement. Motivation provides the drive and energy required to work towards goals, even when facing challenges or setbacks. Intrinsic motivation, which comes from within an individual, is particularly powerful. It's driven by an interest in the task or enjoyment in doing it, rather than external pressures or rewards.

<u>Vision</u> is the ability to imagine your future in a way that inspires you. It creates a picture of what you aspire to achieve and can serve as a source of inspiration during the goal-setting process. A compelling vision helps you understand the purpose behind your goals, which can be a powerful motivator.

Having a clear vision can also help you maintain focus, steer your decision-making, and align your short-term action plans with your long-term objectives. When motivation wanes—as it inevitably can—a strong vision can remind you why you set out on your goal-achieving journey in the first place, rekindling your drive to continue.

Together, motivation and vision create a foundation on which goals are built. They provide the why (vision) and the how (motivation) that are critical for setting goals that are meaningful, engaging, and ultimately, achievable.

Chapter 2: HEALTH –
The Foundation of Success:

Health is not merely the absence of disease or infirmity but a state of complete physical, mental, and social well-being. It is a cornerstone upon which much of our ability to be productive, fulfilled, and successful in life is built. Let's explore how prioritizing health can enhance our overall well-being and productivity and discuss some strategies for integrating healthful practices into our daily routines.

The Importance of Health for Overall Well-Being and Productivity

Health is often likened to the foundation of a house—it supports every aspect of your life. When your health is compromised, it's much harder to focus, achieve goals, or enjoy life. Conversely, when you are healthy, you have the energy and clarity of mind needed to pursue your ambitions and engage with the world around you.

Being in good health enhances your quality of life and can improve your longevity. It also makes you more resilient, allowing you to bounce back more quickly from illness or injury. Additionally, health has a direct impact on productivity. A healthy individual can perform tasks more efficiently, maintain better focus, and generally produces higher-quality work.

Incorporating Exercise into Daily Life

Physical activity is one of the most effective ways to improve health. Exercise has numerous benefits for both the body and the mind, including:

- Strengthening the cardiovascular system.
- Improving muscle and bone strength.
- Enhancing flexibility and balance.
- Boosting mental health by reducing anxiety and depression.
- Sharpening cognitive functions.

Creating a detailed plan for exercise means finding activities you enjoy and can stick with over the long term. **It's recommended to aim for at least 150 minutes of moderate aerobic activity or 75 minutes of vigorous aerobic activity per week, plus muscle-strengthening activities on two or more days per week.**

Nutrition: Fueling Your Success

Nutrition plays a crucial role in health. The food you eat provides the energy and nutrients your body needs to function correctly. A balanced diet helps you maintain a healthy weight, supports your immune system, and reduces the risk of chronic diseases.

To improve your nutrition:

- Eat a variety of fruits and vegetables every day.
- Choose whole grains over refined grains.
- Include lean proteins in your diet.
- Limit added sugars and saturated fats.
- Stay hydrated by drinking plenty of water.

Sleep: The Underrated Health Pillar

Sleep is essential for health and wellbeing. It allows the body to repair and be fit and ready for another day. Good sleep improves learning, memory, mood, and physical health. Aim for 7-9 hours of quality sleep each night. To improve sleep:

- Establish a regular sleep schedule.
- Create a restful sleeping environment.
- Limit exposure to screens before bedtime.
- Avoid caffeine and heavy meals in the evening.

Stress Management: Keeping Balance

Chronic stress can lead to serious health problems. Managing stress is vital for maintaining good health. Techniques for stress management include:

- Regular physical activity.
- Practicing relaxation techniques such as deep breathing, meditation, or yoga.
- Keeping a positive attitude and practicing gratitude.
- Seeking professional help when necessary.

Personal Anecdotes and Success Stories

Many people have transformed their lives by making health a priority. For example, consider the story of a busy executive who, after suffering from stress-induced hypertension, turned to exercise, improved nutrition, and mindfulness practices.

In Summary
Health:
1. **Exercise at least 3 times per week for 30 minutes:**
   - Schedule specific workout times in your weekly calendar.
   - Choose activities you enjoy, such as walking, cycling, or dancing.

- Start with shorter sessions and gradually increase duration and intensity.

2. **Eat at least 5 servings of fruits and vegetables each day**:
   - Plan your meals and snacks to include a variety of fruits and vegetables.
   - Experiment with new recipes and cooking methods to make healthy eating enjoyable.
   - Consider joining a local community-supported agriculture (CSA) program for fresh produce.

3. **Get at least 7-8 hours of sleep each night:**
   - Establish a relaxing bedtime routine to signal to your body that it's time to wind down.
   - Create a comfortable sleep environment by adjusting room temperature and reducing screen time before bed.
   - Consider using sleep tracking apps or devices to monitor your sleep patterns.

4. **Practice stress-reducing activities such as meditation or yoga**:
   - Set aside time each day for mindfulness meditation or deep breathing exercises.
   - Explore different types of yoga classes or online tutorials to find what suits you best.
   - Consider joining a local meditation or yoga group for community support.

5. **Drink at least 8 glasses of water per day:**
   - Carry a reusable water bottle with you to encourage regular hydration.
   - Set reminders on your phone or use an app to track your water intake.
   - Experiment with adding natural flavors, such as lemon or cucumber, to make water more appealing.

Chapter 3: WEALTH–
Securing Your Future:

The Role of Financial Stability in Personal Development

Financial stability plays a crucial role in personal development by providing individuals with a sense of security, freedom, and opportunity. When individuals are financially stable, they are better equipped to pursue their goals, maintain their well-being, and contribute to their communities. Here are some specific ways in which financial stability impacts personal development:

1. **Reduced Stress and Anxiety:** Financial stability can alleviate many of the stressors and anxieties associated with money management, such as living paycheck to paycheck, struggling to pay bills, or dealing with debt. This reduction in stress can lead to improved mental and emotional well-being, allowing individuals to focus on personal growth and development.

2. **Freedom to Pursue Goals:** With financial stability, individuals have the freedom to pursue their passions, education, career advancement, and entrepreneurial endeavors without being hindered by financial constraints. This can lead to greater personal fulfillment and growth.

3. **Enhanced Quality of Life:** Financial stability enables individuals to afford better healthcare, housing, education, and leisure activities, all of which contribute to an improved quality of life. This, in turn, can positively impact personal well-being and development.

4. **Long-Term Planning and Security:** Financial stability provides the foundation for long-term planning, such as saving for retirement, investing in education, or purchasing a home. Having a secure financial future can provide peace of mind and a sense of security, which are essential for personal development.

Step-by-Step Guidance on Budgeting, Saving, Investing, and Debt Management.

1. Budgeting:
   - Start by tracking your income and expenses to understand your financial inflows and outflows.
   - Create a monthly budget that allocates your income to essential expenses (e.g., housing, utilities, groceries), savings, and discretionary spending.
   - Use budgeting tools or apps to help you track your expenses and stay within your budget.

2. Saving:
   - Establish an emergency fund to cover unexpected expenses or financial setbacks. Aim to save three to six months' worth of living expenses.
   - Set specific savings goals, whether it's for a major purchase, a vacation, or long-term objectives like retirement.

3. Investing:
   - Educate yourself about different investment options, such as stocks, bonds, mutual funds, and real estate.
   - Consider your risk tolerance and investment time horizon when selecting investment vehicles.
   - Diversify your investment portfolio to spread risk and potentially enhance returns.

4. Debt Management:
   - Create a plan to pay off high-interest debt, such as credit card debt, as quickly as possible.
   - Prioritize debt with the highest interest rates while making minimum payments on other debts.
   - Consider strategies like debt consolidation or refinancing to lower interest rates and simplify debt repayment.

5. Long-Term Planning:
   - Develop a retirement savings strategy, such as contributing to employer-sponsored retirement plans like 401(k)s or opening individual retirement accounts (IRAs).

- Consider seeking advice from financial professionals to help plan for major life events, such as buying a home or funding a child's education.

Implementing these steps can help individuals establish a solid financial foundation, reduce financial stress, and work toward long-term financial security, ultimately contributing to their overall personal development and well-being.

In Summary
 <u>**Wealth:**</u>
1. **Create and stick to a monthly budget:**
   - Review your income and expenses to create a realistic budget.
   - Use budgeting apps or spreadsheets to track your spending and identify areas for improvement.
   - Schedule regular budget check-ins to assess your progress and adjust.

2. **Save a specific percentage of your income each month:**
   - Set up automatic transfers to a separate savings account to make saving effortless.
   - Consider setting short-term savings goals, such as a vacation or home improvement project, to stay motivated.
   - Research high-yield savings accounts or other investment options to maximize your savings.

3. **Start investing in a retirement account or other long-term savings**:
   - Research different retirement account options, such as 401(k)s or IRAs, and choose the best fit for your situation.
   - Consult with a financial advisor to create an investment strategy aligned with your long-term goals.
   - Regularly review and adjust your investment portfolio based on your risk tolerance and changing market conditions.

4. **Pay off any high-interest debts or loans:**
   - Create a debt repayment plan, prioritizing high-interest debts first.
   - Consider debt consolidation or refinancing options to reduce interest rates.
   - Seek advice from a financial counselor or debt management professional if needed.

5. **Increase your income through a side hustle or additional education:**
   - Identify your skills and interests to explore potential side hustle opportunities.

- Research online courses or certifications to enhance your professional qualifications.
- Network with professionals in your desired industry to discover new career opportunities.

Chapter 4: RELATIONSHIPS- The bonds that shape us:

The Impact of Personal Relationships on Happiness and Success

Personal relationships play a vital role in shaping our happiness and success. Numerous studies have shown that strong and healthy relationships contribute significantly to overall well-being and fulfillment. Positive relationships provide emotional support, reduce stress, and increase our sense of belonging and purpose. In the professional sphere, the quality of our relationships often determines our success. Networking, collaboration, and effective communication are all rooted in building and maintaining strong connections with others. Therefore, understanding the impact of relationships on our lives and learning to nurture them is essential for both personal and professional growth.

Strategies for Improving Communication, Showing Appreciation, and Building Connections

1. **Effective Communication:**
   - Practice active listening: Focus on what the other person is saying without interrupting and provide feedback to demonstrate understanding.
   - Use "I" statements: Express your feelings and thoughts using "I" statements to avoid sounding accusatory or confrontational.
   - Be mindful of non-verbal cues: Pay attention to body language and tone of voice to ensure your communication is consistent with your intended message.

2. **Showing Appreciation:**
   - Express gratitude: Regularly acknowledge and thank others for their contributions, support, or presence in your life.

- Provide positive feedback: Offer specific compliments and praise to show appreciation for others' efforts and qualities.
- Take time for meaningful gestures: Small acts of kindness, such as sending a thoughtful note or helping, can go a long way in expressing appreciation.

3. **Building Connections:**
- Foster empathy: Seek to understand others' perspectives and emotions and show genuine interest in their experiences.
- Create shared experiences: Engage in activities or conversations that strengthen the bond and create lasting memories.
- Invest time in relationships: Dedicate quality time to nurture connections with family, friends, and colleagues.

Exercises for Conflict Resolution and Deepening Relationships

1. **Conflict Resolution:**
- Reflective listening: Each party takes turns expressing their perspective while the other listens without interruption. Then, summarize the other person's viewpoint to ensure understanding.
- Identify common ground: Explore shared goals and values to find areas of agreement and build from there.
- Brainstorm solutions: Collaborate on generating potential solutions, considering the needs and concerns of all parties involved.

2. **Deepening Relationships:**
- Vulnerability exercises: Share personal stories or experiences that reveal your authentic self, fostering deeper connections through mutual trust.
- Relationship visioning: Discuss and envisions the ideal future of the relationship, setting goals and aspirations together.
- Mutual support activities: Engage in activities that support each other's personal growth and well-being, such as exercising together or pursuing shared hobbies.

In conclusion, personal relationships are pivotal to our happiness and success. By honing our communication skills, demonstrating appreciation, and actively working to resolve conflicts and deepen connections, we can cultivate meaningful and fulfilling relationships that enrich our lives in countless ways.

In summary
<u>Relationship:</u>
1. **Schedule regular quality time with your partner/spouse:**
   - Plan date nights or weekend activities in advance to ensure dedicated time together.
   - Alternate decision-making for date ideas to share the responsibility and excitement.
   - Use technology to sync calendars and avoid scheduling conflicts.

2. **Improve communication with your loved ones:**
   - Practice active listening by giving your full attention during conversations.
   - Use "I" statements to express your feelings and avoid placing blame.
   - Schedule regular check-ins to discuss any concerns or celebrate achievements.

3. **Show appreciation for your friends and family regularly:**
   - Send handwritten notes or small gifts to express your gratitude.
   - Plan surprise appreciation events or gatherings to honor your loved ones.
   - Use social media or messaging apps to stay connected and share positive affirmations.

4. **Resolve conflicts through open and honest discussions:**
   - Establish a safe and neutral environment for discussions to take place.
   - Use "time-outs" if emotions run high and agree to revisit the conversation later.
   - Seek professional help, such as couples counseling, if necessary.

5. **Initiate and cultivate new friendships or social connections:**
   - Attend social events or join clubs and groups aligned with your interests.
   - Host gatherings or casual meetups to introduce potential new friends to your existing social circle.
   - Follow up with new acquaintances and schedule future hangouts to nurture growing friendships.

Chapter 5: CAREER – Crafting Your Path:

Emphasizing Career Planning and Professional Growth

Career planning and professional growth are essential for achieving personal fulfillment and success in the professional realm. By actively shaping one's career path and continuously developing skills, individuals can maximize their potential and create meaningful impact in their chosen field. Here are key aspects to consider:

1. Career Planning:
   - Self-assessment: Reflect on personal values, strengths, interests, and long-term aspirations to identify potential career paths.
   - Setting goals: Establish short-term and long-term career objectives, considering factors such as job satisfaction, financial security, and work-life balance.
   - Continuous learning: Stay informed about industry trends, emerging technologies, and evolving job market demands to adapt and grow within one's career trajectory.

2. Professional Growth:
   - Skill development: Identify and cultivate both technical and soft skills relevant to one's career goals, considering areas such as leadership, communication, and adaptability.
   - Seeking mentorship: Engage with experienced professionals who can offer guidance, advice, and support in navigating career challenges and opportunities.
   - Embracing change: Remain open to new opportunities, challenges, and experiences that foster personal and professional growth.

Advice on Education, Skill Development, Networking, and Work-Life Balance

1.Education and Skill Development:
   - Lifelong learning: Pursue formal education, certifications, or specialized training to enhance expertise and adapt to industry demands.

- Online resources: Leverage online courses, webinars, and educational platforms to acquire new skills and stay updated on industry best practices.
- Cross-functional knowledge: Seek opportunities to diversify skills by exploring complementary disciplines or fields of study.

2. **Networking:**
- Building professional relationships: Actively engage with peers, mentors, and industry leaders to expand professional networks and gain insights from diverse perspectives.
- Utilizing social media: Leverage professional networking platforms, such as LinkedIn, to connect with like-minded professionals and stay informed about industry news and opportunities.
- Attending industry events: Participate in conferences, workshops, and seminars to network with industry peers and stay current on industry trends.

3. **Work-Life Balance:**
- Setting boundaries: Establish clear boundaries between work and personal life to maintain overall well-being and prevent burnout.
- Prioritizing self-care: Dedicate time to activities that promote mental and physical health, such as exercise, hobbies, and relaxation.
- Effective time management: Develop strategies to manage time efficiently and prioritize tasks to maintain a healthy work-life balance.

<u>Interviews or Case Studies of Successful Career Advancements</u>

In this chapter, it would be beneficial to include interviews or case studies of individuals who have achieved successful career advancements through strategic planning and continuous growth. These interviews or case studies can provide valuable insights into the experiences, challenges, and strategies that have propelled individuals to career success. Hearing firsthand from professionals who have navigated the complexities of career development can inspire and guide readers as they craft their own career paths.

In conclusion, by emphasizing career planning, continuous professional growth, and the importance of education, skill development, networking, and work-life balance, individuals can proactively shape their careers and achieve long-term success and fulfillment. Incorporating real-world examples and insights from successful professionals can further enrich the chapter and provide actionable guidance for readers.

In Summary
<u>**Career:**</u>
1. **Set clear career advancement goals for the year:**
   - Identify specific skills or experiences you need to achieve your career goals.
   - Create a career development plan with measurable milestones and timelines.
   - Schedule regular progress reviews to assess your advancement and adjust your plan as needed.

2. **Pursue additional training or education to enhance your skills:**
   - Research online courses, workshops, or certifications relevant to your field.
   - Seek employer-sponsored training programs or tuition reimbursement opportunities.
   - Network with professionals in your industry to gather recommendations for valuable learning resources.

3. **Seek out a mentor or career coach to guide you:**
   - Identify potential mentors within your organization or industry and reach out to them.
   - Prepare specific questions and topics for mentorship meetings to maximize their value.
   - Express gratitude and provide updates on your progress to maintain a healthy mentor-mentee relationship.

4. **Network with professionals in your industry:**
   - Attend industry conferences, trade shows, or networking events to meet new contacts.
   - Utilize professional networking platforms, such as LinkedIn, to connect with like-minded individuals.
   - Follow up with new contacts to nurture relationships and seek collaboration opportunities.

5. **Improve time management and productivity at work:**
   - Analyze your current workflow to identify time-wasting activities or inefficiencies.

- Implement time management techniques, such as the Pomodoro Technique or time blocking, to increase productivity.
- Prioritize tasks based on urgency and importance to maximize your work output.

Chapter 6: SPIRITUALITY – The Inner Journey:

The Importance of Spiritual Well-Being and Its Influence on Other Life Areas

Spirituality plays a significant role in shaping individuals' overall well-being, influencing their emotional, mental, and even physical health. It encompasses a sense of connection to something greater than oneself and can provide meaning, purpose, and a sense of inner peace. Here are the key aspects to explore:

1. **Emotional and Mental Well-Being:**
   - Spirituality often serves as a source of comfort during challenging times, providing individuals with a sense of hope, resilience, and inner strength.
   - It can contribute to emotional stability and help individuals navigate feelings of anxiety, stress, or grief by providing a sense of perspective and purpose.

2. **Relationships and Community:**
   - Spiritual beliefs and practices can foster a sense of community and connectedness, providing individuals with a support network and a sense of belonging.
   - Spirituality can influence how individuals approach relationships, empathy, and compassion, thereby shaping their interactions with others.

3. **Personal Growth and Meaning:**
   - Spirituality can serve as a guiding force in individuals' pursuit of personal growth, self-discovery, and the search for meaning and purpose in life.

- It often encourages individuals to reflect on their values, ethics, and the impact of their actions, leading to a deeper understanding of themselves and their place in the world.

Guidance for Meditation, Mindfulness, and Community Involvement

1. Meditation and Mindfulness:
   - Meditation practices: Introduce various meditation techniques, such as mindfulness meditation, loving-kindness meditation, and body scan meditation, to promote emotional regulation and mental clarity.
   - Cultivating mindfulness: Offer guidance on integrating mindfulness into daily activities, fostering present-moment awareness, and reducing stress.

2. **Community Involvement**:
   - Engaging with spiritual communities: Encourage participation in religious or spiritual groups, meditation circles, or community service organizations to foster a sense of belonging and shared purpose.
   - Acts of service: Highlight the value of volunteer work and community involvement as a means of expressing compassion and contributing to the well-being of others.

Sharing Personal Spiritual Journeys or Others' Experiences

Sharing personal spiritual journeys or the experiences of others can provide valuable insights and inspiration for readers. These stories can illustrate the diverse paths individuals take in their spiritual pursuits and highlight the transformative impact of spirituality on their lives. Hearing about real-life experiences can offer guidance and encouragement to those who are exploring their own spiritual journeys.

In sharing personal experiences, it's important to convey authenticity, vulnerability, and the lessons learned along the way. Additionally, featuring diverse perspectives and spiritual traditions can help readers appreciate the richness and universality of the human spiritual experience.

In conclusion, exploring the significance of spiritual well-being and its influence on various aspects of life, providing guidance for meditation, mindfulness, and community involvement, and sharing personal spiritual journeys or the experiences of others can help individuals cultivate a deeper sense of purpose, connectedness, and inner peace in their lives.

In Summary
Spiritual:
1. **Establish a daily meditation or mindfulness practice**:   - Start with short sessions and gradually increase the duration as you become more comfortable.
   - Create a designated space for meditation, free from distractions and conducive to relaxation.
   - Explore different meditation techniques, such as mindfulness, loving-kindness, or guided meditation.

2. **Read and reflect on spiritual or philosophical texts**:
   - Set aside dedicated time each day or week for reading and contemplation.
   - Keep a journal to record your thoughts, insights, and questions arising from your readings.
   - Join a book club or discussion group focused on spiritual and philosophical literature.

3. **Connect with a community that shares your spiritual beliefs**:
   - Research local religious or spiritual organizations to find a community aligned with your beliefs.
   - Attend services, gatherings, or events to meet like-minded individuals and build connections.
   - Volunteer to contribute to the community and deepen your sense of belonging.

4. **Volunteer for a cause you are passionate about**:
   - Identify local charitable organizations or community initiatives aligned with your values.
   - Offer your time, skills, or resources to support causes that resonate with you.
   - Engage in volunteer activities that promote compassion, empathy, and social justice.

5. **Engage in acts of kindness and compassion**:
   - Practice random acts of kindness, such as helping a neighbor or complimenting a stranger.
   - Volunteer for community service projects or charitable events to make a positive impact.
   - Cultivate a mindset of empathy and compassion in your daily interactions with others.

Chapter 7: Bringing It All Together

Integrating goals across different life domains is essential for creating a sense of balance and fulfillment. A holistic approach to goal setting involves considering various aspects of life, such as career, health, relationships, personal development, and leisure. Here's a guide to help you integrate and pursue your goals effectively:

Integrating Goals Across Different Life Domains

1. **Identify Key Life Domains:** Start by identifying the key areas of your life that are important to you. This may include career, health, relationships, personal growth, leisure, and spirituality, among others.

2. **Set Specific Goals for Each Domain:** Within each domain, set specific, measurable, achievable, relevant, and time-bound (SMART) goals. For example, in the career domain, your goal might be to get a promotion within the next 12 months, while in the health domain, it could be to exercise at least three times a week.

3. **Look for Interconnections:** Explore how goals in different domains might complement or conflict with each other. For instance, pursuing a demanding career goal might require adjustments in your personal life to maintain balance.

4. **Align Goals with Values:** Ensure that your goals align with your core values and beliefs. This will help bring coherence to your overall life plan.

Importance of Balance and Flexibility in Goal Pursuit

1. **Strive for Balance:** Aim to distribute your time and energy across different life domains to avoid neglecting any important aspect of your life.

2. **Be Flexible:** Life is dynamic, and circumstances change. It's crucial to remain adaptable and open to adjusting your goals as needed to accommodate changes in your life circumstances.

3. **Prioritize Self-Care:** Recognize the importance of self-care and well-being in achieving your goals. Taking care of your physical and mental health should be a priority.

Yearly or Monthly Plan for Goal Achievement

1. **Yearly Planning:**
   - At the beginning of the year, review your life domains and set specific, achievable goals for each.
   - Create a timeline for each goal, breaking them down into manageable steps.
   - Schedule regular check-ins throughout the year to track your progress and adjust as needed.

2. **Monthly Planning:**
   - At the beginning of each month, review your yearly goals and break them down into monthly targets.
   - Allocate time in your schedule for activities related to each goal.
   - Reflect on your progress at the end of the month and make any necessary adjustments to your plan.

3. **Regular Reflection and Adjustment:**
   - Set aside time on a weekly or bi-weekly basis to reflect on your progress and reassess your goals.

- Be open to making changes based on what you've learned and experienced.
    - Celebrate your achievements and learn from any setbacks.

By integrating goals across different life domains, maintaining balance, and being flexible in your approach, you can create a comprehensive plan for personal growth and fulfillment. Regular reflection and adjustment are key to staying on track and adapting to the evolving nature of life.

Chapter 8: Overcoming Obstacles

Overcoming obstacles is an essential part of achieving any goal, and it often requires a combination of perseverance, motivation, and resilience. Here are some strategies for addressing common challenges and setbacks in goal achievement, staying motivated, overcoming procrastination, and dealing with failure:

Addressing Common Challenges and Setbacks in Goal Achievement:

1. **Identify Potential Obstacles:** Anticipate potential challenges that may arise on the path to achieving your goal. This can include lack of resources, time constraints, or unforeseen circumstances.

2. **Develop a Contingency Plan:** Create a plan for how you will address these obstacles if they arise. Having a contingency plan in place can help you stay on track when faced with setbacks.

3. **Seek Support:** Don't be afraid to ask for help when facing challenges. Whether it's seeking advice from a mentor, collaborating with a colleague, or finding a supportive community, having a support network can make a significant difference.

4. **Stay Flexible:** Be willing to adjust your approach if necessary. Sometimes, the path to achieving a goal may need to change due to unforeseen obstacles. Adaptability is key to overcoming setbacks.

Strategies for Staying Motivated and Overcoming Procrastination:

1. **Set Clear Milestones:** Break your goal down into smaller, manageable tasks and celebrate your progress along the way. This can help you stay motivated by providing a sense of accomplishment.

2. **Visualize Success:** Regularly visualize yourself successfully achieving your goal. This can help reinforce your motivation and keep your focus on the end result.

3. **Find Inspiration:** Surround yourself with sources of inspiration, whether it's motivational quotes, success stories, or supportive individuals who believe in your abilities.

4. **Establish a Routine:** Create a routine that incorporates regular progress toward your goal. Consistency can help prevent procrastination and maintain motivation.

5. **Address Procrastination:** If you find yourself procrastinating, identify the underlying reasons and address them. Whether it's fear of failure, perfectionism, or feeling overwhelmed, understanding the root cause can help you overcome procrastination.

Dealing with Failure and Learning from Experiences:

1. **Embrace a Growth Mindset:** View failures as opportunities for growth and learning. Embracing a growth mindset can help you see setbacks as temporary and motivates you to keep moving forward.

2. **Reflect on the Experience:** Take time to reflect on what led to the setback or failure. Identify lessons learned and consider how you can apply these insights to future endeavors.

3. **Seek Feedback:** Reach out to trusted individuals for constructive feedback. Their perspectives can offer valuable insights and help you gain a different perspective on the situation.

4. **Stay Resilient:** Resilience is key to bouncing back from failure. Remind yourself of your strengths and past achievements to bolster your confidence.

5. **Reassess and Adjust:** Use your experiences to reassess your goals and strategies. Adjust your approach as needed, considering the lessons learned from past setbacks.

Remember that challenges and setbacks are a natural part of any journey toward achieving a goal. By staying motivated, seeking support, and learning from your experiences, you can overcome obstacles and continue making progress toward your aspirations.

Chapter 9: Tools and Resources

Apps for Goal Setting and Productivity:

1. **Todoist:** A popular task management app that helps you organize your tasks, set deadlines, and track your progress.

2. **Trello**: A visual collaboration tool that allows you to organize and prioritize your projects using boards, lists, and cards.

3. **Habitica:** An app that gamifies goal setting and habit tracking, turning your tasks into a role-playing game.

4. **Forest:** This app helps you stay focused and avoid distractions by growing virtual trees as you work. It's a great tool for improving productivity.

5. **Strides:** A powerful tracking app that enables you to set and track goals, habits, and targets in various areas of your life.

Books for Motivation and Personal Development:

1. **"The Power of Habit"** by *Charles Duhigg*: This book explores the science behind habits and how they can be transformed to achieve success.

2. **"Grit: The Power of Passion and Perseverance"** by *Angela Duckworth*: Duckworth discusses the role of perseverance and passion in achieving long-term goals.

3. **"Atomic Habits"** by *James Clear*: Clear provides practical strategies for building good habits, breaking bad ones, and mastering the tiny behaviors that lead to remarkable results.

4. **"Mindset: The New Psychology of Success"** by *Carol S. Dweck*: This book explores the concept of a growth mindset and its impact on achieving success.

5. **"The 7 Habits of Highly Effective People"** by *Stephen R. Covey*: Covey's classic book offers a holistic approach to personal and interpersonal effectiveness.

Websites and Online Communities:

1. **Coursera**: Offers a wide range of online courses on goal setting, productivity, and personal development, often taught by experts in the field.

2. **Lifehacker:** A popular website offering tips and tricks for maximizing productivity, time management, and personal development.

3. **Reddit:** Subreddits such as r/Get Motivated and r/DecidingToBeBetter can be valuable sources of inspiration, advice, and support from like-minded individuals.

4. **MindTools**: Provides resources for essential skills in management, leadership, and personal effectiveness, including articles, worksheets, and interactive tools.

Role of Technology in Tracking and Supporting Goal Progress:

Technology plays a significant role in facilitating goal tracking and providing support for goal achievement. Here's how technology can help:

1. **Tracking Progress**: Apps and digital tools provide easy ways to track your progress toward goals, whether it's through task lists, habit tracking, or goal-specific metrics.

2. **Automation**: Technology can automate routine tasks, freeing up time and mental energy to focus on goal-related activities.

3. **Data Analysis:** By leveraging technology, individuals can analyze their progress and identify patterns, allowing for informed decision-making and adjustments to their strategies.

4. **Community and Support:** Online communities and social platforms provide opportunities to connect with others pursuing similar goals, offering encouragement, advice, and accountability.

5. **Accessibility:** With the widespread use of smartphones and other devices, goal-setting tools and resources are more accessible than ever, allowing individuals to stay connected to their goals on the go.

Conclusion

Congratulations on embarking on the journey toward achieving your goals! Remember, the first step is often the most challenging, but it is also the most important. By taking that initial step, you are demonstrating your commitment to your aspirations and setting the stage for meaningful progress. As you move forward, keep in mind that every small step you take brings you closer to your desired outcome.

The abundance of apps, books, websites, and technology tools available today provides individuals with a wealth of resources to support their goal setting and achievement efforts.

In the words of _Lao Tzu_, **"The journey of a thousand miles begins with one step."** Embrace this wisdom as you pursue your goals and remember that even the smallest actions can lead to significant results. Stay focused, remain resilient in the face of challenges, and always believe in your ability to overcome obstacles. Your determination and perseverance will carry you through any setbacks that may arise.

Final Words of Motivation and Wisdom

As you continue your journey, remember that the pursuit of your goals is not just about reaching a destination—it's also about the growth, learning, and self-discovery that occur along the way. Embrace the process, celebrate your progress, and be compassionate with yourself during moments of difficulty. Each experience, whether a victory or a setback, offers valuable lessons and opportunities for personal development.

The path to achieving your goals may not always be smooth, but it is undoubtedly worthwhile. Your dedication, combined with the knowledge and strategies you've acquired, will propel you forward. Trust in your abilities, stay true to your vision, and let your passion be the guiding force that propels you toward success.

Remember, you have the power to shape your future and create the life you envision. Keep moving forward with determination, and never underestimate the impact of your efforts. You can achieve remarkable things, and your journey toward your goals is a testament to your strength and resilience.

Appendices

Templates for Goal Setting and Tracking
- Goal Setting Worksheet
- Habit Tracking Template
- Project Planning Template

Checklists for Daily, Weekly, and Monthly Goal Review
- Daily Reflection Checklist
- Weekly Progress Review Checklist
- Monthly Goal Assessment Checklist

Inspirational Quotes or Affirmations for Each Category
- "Believe you can and you're halfway there." – Theodore Roosevelt
- "Success is the sum of small efforts repeated day in and day out." – Robert Collier
- "The only limit to our realization of tomorrow will be our doubts of today." – Franklin D. Roosevelt

References

The content of this book was informed by a wide range of research, expert insights, and literature, including but not limited to:

- Scientific studies on goal setting and achievement
- Works by experts in psychology, personal development, and productivity
- Articles from reputable publications and academic journals

Book Writing Tips:

Personal Touch

Incorporate personal anecdotes, stories, and testimonies to make the content relatable and engaging for readers. Real-life examples can inspire and provide practical insights.

Actionable Content

Ensure that each chapter offers actionable advice and steps that readers can immediately implement in their own lives. Practical guidance is key to empowering readers to take meaningful action.

Visual Elements

Integrate visual elements such as charts, graphs, and images to enhance the presentation of information and provide a visually engaging experience for readers. Visual aids can help break up text and reinforce key points.

As you finalize your book, remember that your words have the potential to inspire, empower, and guide others toward achieving their goals.

www.ingramcontent.com/pod-product-compliance
Lightning Source LLC
Chambersburg PA
CBHW070236260726
48658CB00006BA/2360